Shadows

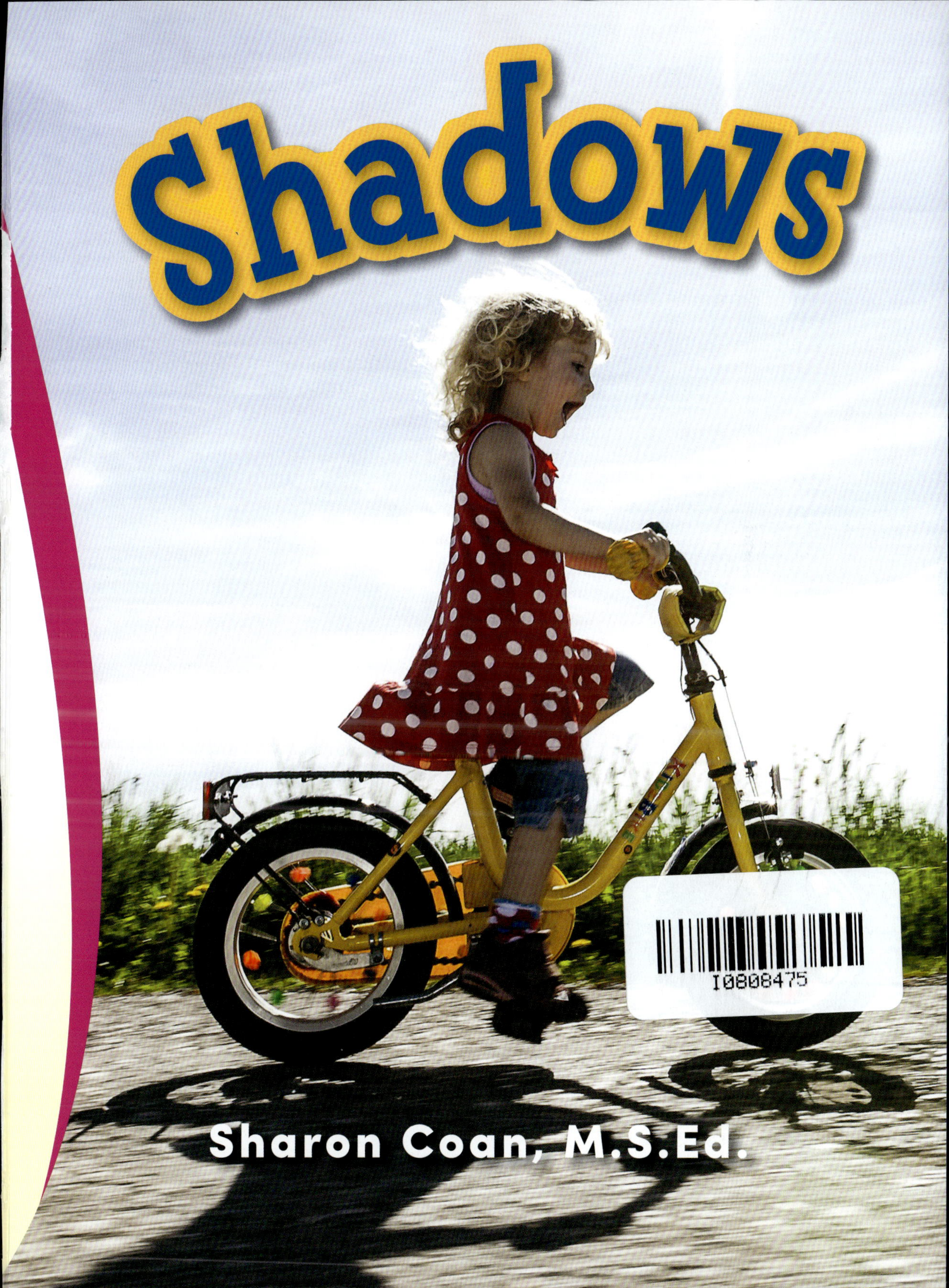

Sharon Coan, M.S.Ed.

Consultants

Sally Creel, Ed.D.
Curriculum Consultant

Leann Iacuone, M.A.T., NBCT, ATC
Riverside Unified School District

Jill Tobin
California Teacher of the Year
Semi-Finalist
Burbank Unified School District

Image Credits: Cover & p.1 Wilfried Feder/agefotostock; p.13 Stuart Pearce/agefotostock; p.14 Tokyo Space Club/agefotostock; p.10 Trip/agefotostock; p.22 UFO RFa Collection/agefotostock; p.9 Cultura Creative/Alamy; p.7 Image Source/Alamy; p.6 Tim Gainey/Alamy; p.5 Getty Images/Flickr; p.19 Photo and Co/Getty Images; pp.2, 3 majorosl/iStock; all other images from Shutterstock.

Library of Congress Cataloging-in-Publication Data

Coan, Sharon, author.
Shadows / Sharon Coan, M.S.Ed.; consultants, Sally Creel, Ed.D., curriculum consultant, Leann Iacuone, M.A.T., NBCT, ATC Riverside Unified School District, Jill Tobin, California Teacher of the Year Semi-Finalist, Burbank Unified School District.
pages cm
Summary: "Have you seen your shadow today? It follows you around. Shadows can change shapes and sizes. What else has a shadow?"— Provided by publisher.
Audience: K to grade 3.
Includes index.
ISBN 978-1-4807-4567-4 (pbk.)
ISBN 978-1-4807-5057-9 (ebook)
1. Shades and shadows—Juvenile literature. I. Title.
QC381.6.C63 2015
535.4—dc23
2014013153

Teacher Created Materials
5301 Oceanus Drive
Huntington Beach, CA 92649-1030
http://www.tcmpub.com

ISBN 978-1-4807-4567-4

Printed by: 51497
Printed in: Taiwan

Table of Contents

Good Morning!

The sun rises.

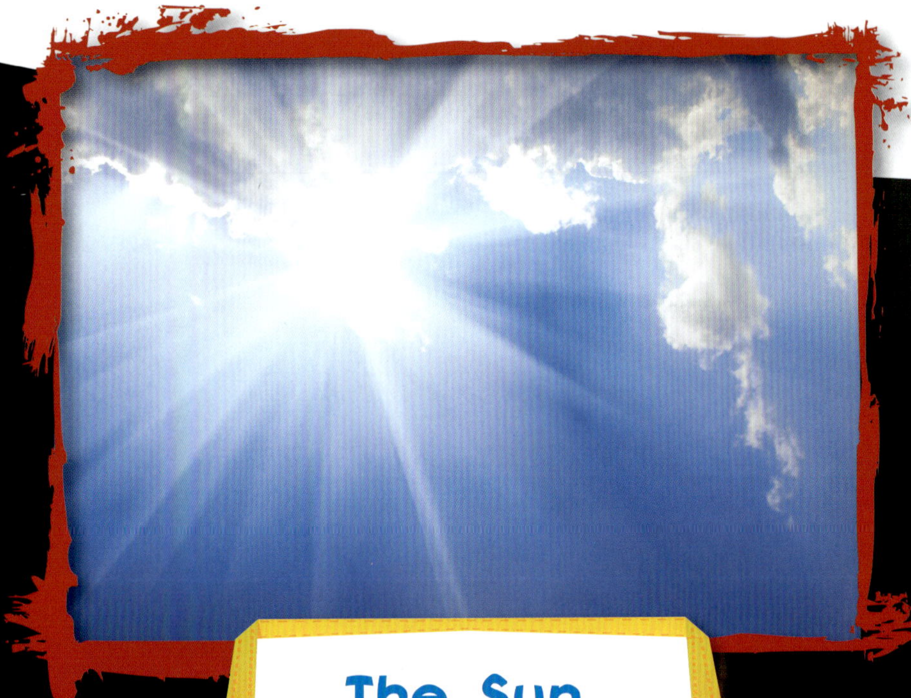

The Sun

The sun is a star. It gives us light and heat.

Its **light** comes in my window.

It **shines** on me.

But it cannot shine through me.

The sun makes my **shadow appear** on the wall.

In the morning, shadows look tall.

Shadows Are Everywhere

Later, we go to school.

The sun appears higher in the sky. Shadows are shorter.

After lunch, we play outside.

The sun is high in the sky. So shadows are very short.

After school, we go home.

The sun appears to have moved across the sky.

My shadow is on the other side.

It is getting taller again.

Good Night!

Now, it is night. The sun has set.

I need a **lamp** to make my shadow.

Let's Do Science!

How does moving a light source affect a shadow? Try this and see!

What to Get

- flashlight
- object to make a shadow
- paper and pencil

What to Do

1. Place your object on a table. Darken the lights in the room where you are working.

2. Shine the flashlight on your object from different directions. What do you see?

3. Can you make the shadow long or short? Can you move the shadow to a different side?

4. Draw pictures to show your work. Show how the light shines on the object. Look at all your pictures. What do you notice?

Glossary

appear—can be seen

lamp—an object that makes light

light—energy that helps us see things

shadow—dark area made when an object blocks light

shines—glows with light

Index

Your Turn!

Finding Shadows

Look for shadows. Look for where the light is coming from. Look for the object that is making the shadow. Keep a list of objects that make interesting shadows.